Snowflake Ch

5

CORPORATE VIRTUE SIGNALLING:

How to Stop Big Business
from Meddling in Politics

JEREMY SAMMUT

CULTURE, PROSPERITY
CIVIL SOCIETY
Defending Liberty in Australia

Connor Court Publishing

1
Right thinking on Abortion
Nicola Wright

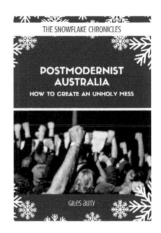

2
Postmodernist Australia
Giles Auty

3
Euthanaisa: Putting the Culture to Death
Peter Kurti

4
Climate Hysteria
Mark Lawson

The Snowflake Chronicles

A word from the publisher

The Snowflake Chronicles book series is an initiative dedicated to pushing the limits of political correctness.

The literary world has become the bastion of progressive thinking that limits free speech and limits topics that were once the norm. The first book of the series was on Abortion. Try talking about Abortion, from a pro-life perspective in academia or even on campuses. It is unthinkable. How many publishers actively publish books that give a pro-life perspective? Are they allowed to? Such is the state of the debate that some topics are purely off-limit, even in a discussion, especially in the world of publishing. So it is in this void that the Snowflake Chronicles were born. We are not snowflakes, we will not crumble or dissolve by listening to an argument. Topics like Abortion, Euthanasia, Coal, Climate Change, Marriage, the minimum wage, immigration, and culture are not topics where the debate has moved on, leaving us behind. We want to bring these topics back from their extinction and show that these so-called contrarian views have merit and will be debated, promoted and encouraged.

So if you are a snowflake, please use these books as a therapy for your recovery. These books will hopefully enlighten the so-called progressive thinker and in some cases cure them. For those who agree with the sentiments of the books, you may find them inspiring and entertaining. Can we encourage you, after you, read them, to help save the world by passing the book onto a snowflake.

Snowflake

A very sensitive person. Someone who is easily hurt or offended by the statements or actions of others.

Published in 2019 by Connor Court Publishing Pty Ltd

Connor Court Publishing Pty Ltd
PO Box 7257
Redland Bay QLD 4165

sales@connorcourt.com
www.connorcourtpublishing.com.au

Phone 0497 900 685

ISBN: 978 1925826432

Cover arrangement Nicola Wright

Front Cover Photo: Karla Pincott

Printed in Australia

contrarian

adjective
1. opposing or rejecting popular opinion or current practice.

1

Introduction

The Turpitude of the Banks

On 4 February 2019, the Royal Commission into misconduct in the banking, superannuation and financial services industry delivered its damning final report. During 11 months of hearings, the Royal Commission headed by former High Court Justice Kenneth Hayne exposed the widespread practice of charging customer fees for financial planning services that were never provided. Revelations of corporate misbehaviour in pursuit of profit have stained the reputations of virtually all the nation's largest and hitherto most trusted financial institutions, including AMP and all of the 'Big Four' banks — NAB, CBA, ANZ and Westpac.[1]

The Royal Commissioner was pointed in condemning the behaviour of the banks and other financial institutions that had taken customers' money under false pretences. Hayne concluded that the unethical conduct and culture exposed in the finance sector had egregiously breached basic community standards and expectations of fairness and honesty as understood by the ordinary person.[2]

In response, Hayne made 76 recommendations proposing changes to laws and practices, which if implemented are expected to lead to increased regulatory and compliance costs for customers and shareholders.[3] Hayne also referred 24 alleged civil and criminal breaches of the law for potential prosecution of institutions including against three of the four big banks.[4] The immediate fallout for the banks precipitated the resignations of NAB chairman Ken Henry and CEO Andrew Thorburn; the less than contrite and accountable attitudes they displayed as witnesses before the Royal Commission was singled out for heavy criticism by Hayne, who questioned both men's willingness to "learn the lessons of the past" and ensure the "right thing" would be done in the future.[5]

Prior to the final reports release, shareholders of the banks — which had traded below long term valuation and had allocated $2.5 billion to fund compensation payments — had already signalled their displeasure. This took the form of an investor revolt at the ANZ, Westpac and NAB annual general meetings, where first strike rejections were recorded against all three company remuneration reports. Shareholders thereby sent a loud and clear — and entirely reasonable — message: in order to earn their generous salaries and bonuses, CEOs and other executives must fulfil their core business duty to provide customers with the reputable, quality services that add real value to company's share prices.[6]

The 'fee for no service' scandal has done great damage to the reputation of corporate Australia. Yet the failure of the banks to fulfil their basic business obligations to customers and shareholders has occurred at a time when they, along with other major corporations, are undertaking an increasing range of so-called 'Corporate Social Responsibility' (CSR) activities.[7]

A standard rationale for CSR — which now appears ironic in the wake of the fate of the banks — has been that simply making profits in an ethical manner is no longer enough. Instead, corporate reputations need to be enhanced by demonstrating that companies are 'not just all about business', an expansive rationale which has led in recent times to companies publicly supporting a range of socially 'progressive' and 'inclusive' causes such as same-sex marriage, climate change, gender diversity and Indigenous Reconciliation.[8]

Corporate Social Responsibility

There is no agreement about the meaning, scope, and content of CSR and the range of company activities that occur under this label. But in general, CSR is based on the belief that for corporations to hold a (unwritten) 'social licence' to operate, companies must fulfil a range of social obligations beyond the traditional profit-making role and duties of limited liability

3

companies. These traditional obligations are to serve the public good by undertaking beneficial economic and entrepreneurial activities and maximise returns on capital for shareholders.

CSR obligations extend beyond compliance with the letter and spirit of relevant company and other laws, and ethical business standards and practices. CSR obligations are generally seen to entail ensuring that corporate decision-making considers the social impacts of company activities on the interests of the wider groups of 'stakeholders' in the community who can be reasonably or legitimately considered affected by those activities.

According to one prominent proponent of corporate involvement in social and political debates in the name of CSR — Alan Joyce, the CEO of Qantas — such involvement is justified because "social issues are very important for all of your stakeholders and are very important for this country."[9] Led by Joyce, Qantas was one of the first major companies to support a 'Yes' vote at the 'marriage equality' plebiscite (the postal survey) held in November 2018.[10] Joyce argued that because they play a "role in the community beyond selling it things," companies "absolutely should" support and speak out on important issues "that ultimately shape what kind of society we live in."

> Let's be clear. A company's first responsibility is to its shareholders and delivering sustainable returns on their investment. To do that, you're automatically part of the community you operate in. Society is your customer base. And just because there is

money changing hands doesn't mean it is only ever an economic transaction. There's an implicit social contract between companies and communities.[11]

This somewhat circular and abstract justification for companies having a broader social remit — they are part of society; therefore, companies should speak out about society — reflects the rationale for CSR. This maintains that the business of business is no longer simply business — or no longer simply a matter of giving primacy to shareholder's interests alone and maximising returns on investments in an ethical manner.[12] According to another prominent corporate leader and proponent of CSR, Paula Dwyer, the chair of gaming giant Tabcorp:

> The community is demanding more of their business leaders and expects them to model behaviour which is constructive for all of society. The role of commerce has to be balanced with the role of companies in the community and part of that is how people behave and act, and what they value.[13]

Public attention in Australia has only recently started to focus on the CSR activities of big business, and mainly in response to the prominent and unprecedented part leading companies (including all four of the big banks[14]) played in the same-sex marriage debate. The campaign to legalise same-sex marriage led by the Australia Marriage Equality lobby group ultimately gained the backing of a reported 1300 Australian businesses that agreed to have their logos published in a show of support.

Hence a common perception is that involvement by corporations in social issues in the name of CSR is a recent phenomenon. In reality, the growing range of CSR activities undertaken by Australian companies is a product of decades of evolution and the development of an extensive international body of corporate management thought and practice concerning the social role of modern corporations since at least the 1950s. (See Chapter 2)

Nevertheless, much of the recent critical attention paid to CSR has focused — with good reason — on accusing business elites of indulging in corporate virtue signalling: of abusing their company's brands to indulge in gratuitous political diversions from their core business of protecting shareholder's financial interests in favour of meddling in politically-contentious social debates.[15]

Big business backing of so-called progressive causes is also the reason why the condemnation of the banks by the Hayne Royal Commission has been greeted with a certain perverse pleasure among more conservative members of the community: corporate titans that signalled their virtue on social issues in the political realm have had their moral feet of clay exposed in the domain of business.[16]

More generally, the damage inflicted on the corporate reputations of the banks and other financial institutions by the financial advice scandal has been compounded by the perception and reality of companies exploiting customers and ignoring basic business ethics and commercial standards, while preoccupying themselves with 'progressive' social agendas.

These companies have been called out for hypocrisy for promoting their commitment to gender diversity and other acts of corporate social responsibility.[17]

The focus on gender quotas in the financial services sector — consistent with the targets endorsed by both the Australian Institute of Company Directors and Australian Stock Exchange, which call for female directors to be appointed to 30% of seats on boards of the top 200 ASX-listed companies by 2020[18] — has been widely criticised as a diversion of board and management attention from the core business of serving customers and protecting shareholder's investments.[19,20]

Just the Tip of the Politicisation of Companies

Therefore, the hope may be that Australian business is now more aware of the risks of leaping into social debates in the name of CSR; and may be more reluctant to tempt fate by presenting companies as the moral arbiters of the nation.

However, in February 2019, mining giants BHP and Rio Tinto became the first major companies to publicly support the Uluru Statement from the Heart, and endorse enshrining an Indigenous 'voice to parliament' in the constitution.[21] According to chief executive Andrew McKenzie, BHP could no longer simply "stand on the sidelines" of the Reconciliation debate and instead the company will take an active part in addressing the "unfinished business with the Indigenous peoples of Australia" by donating $1 million of shareholders' money to support the Recognition campaign.[22]

In a similar vein, a group of leading company directors — including Simon McKeon, Diane Smith-Gander, Jane Hemstrich and Cameron Clyne — have also announced the formation of a new network to encourage business to take the lead on what the Australian Financial Review tellingly called "this year's same-sex marriage debate" and support the push for a republic.[23]

The renewed corporate politicking over Recognition and the republic suggests that those who thought corporate virtue signalling by companies couldn't get any worse than witnessed during the same-sex marriage plebiscite, had better think again. The way big business backed the 'Yes' campaign exposed just the tip of the corporate political meddling that increasing numbers of business leaders believe is justified in the name of CSR.

The apparent readiness of leading corporate figures to encourage companies to not merely blur, but brazenly cross, the line between politics and business by participating in politically-charged debates that are unrelated to core business concerns, reflects the radical ideas that are being promoted by the proponents of CSR inside business. (See Chapter 3)

The Activism and Influence of 'Social Responsibility' Professionals

The aims and objectives of the influential and strategically-placed 'industry' of CSR professionals who now operate within the corporate landscape, speak of the subversion of companies from traditional business endeavours towards naked political activism on issues that have little to do with the true business of business. The army of managers and consultants employed in HR, 'people and culture' and corporate affairs divisions, and in the major professional services firms, that shape CSR policies, are actively — and clearly effectively — pushing for companies to become key participants in driving 'systemic change' around contentious social, environmental, and economic issues.

CSR principles are shaping thought and practice concerning the social role of corporations in Australia at the highest levels of Australian business. This was illustrated by the revised corporate governance standards proposed by the Australian Stock Exchange's (ASX) Corporate Governance Council in May 2018. The proposed new standards sought to cement CSR principles at the heart of Australian business by recognising "the fundamental importance of a listed entity's social license to operate and the need for it to act lawfully, ethically and in a socially responsible manner in order to preserve that license."[24]

Even more significantly, the draft guidelines also contained prescriptive commentary which suggested that in order to earn a 'license', companies would be required to act 'socially responsibly'

9

with regards to inherently politically contentious issues including avoiding tax minimisation, respecting human rights, disclosing climate change risk, paying a living wage, and meeting a range of diversity targets across companies.[25]

The requirement for a 'social license to operate' was dropped from the guidelines in February 2019, but the proposal clearly reflected the activist mindset, ambitions, and influence of the CSR industry. If the CSR activists in Australian business get their way and achieve their objective, they will subvert companies from their traditional roles and functions, and transform the business of business into politics.

Beyond a 'Culture War' Account

As noted, much of the debate about CSR in Australia has been provoked by concerns about 'politically correct' corporations failing to "stick to their knitting" and playing cultural politics with company brands and shareholders' money.[26]

Not surprisingly, corporate involvement in social debates has led to companies such as Qantas being heavily criticised for becoming active political players in the 'culture war' under the rubric of CSR — and hardly without valid reasons. (See, for example, the controversy over the 'inclusive language' information pack issued to all employees by the Qantas People and Culture Group as part of the company's Spirit of Inclusion Month in March 2018.[27])

Much of the critical commentary about CSR has therefore amounted to a polarised account of the phenomenon — with the standard analysis being that corporations have simply become another institution that has been 'captured' or 'marched through' by the Left.[28] This commentary has rightly generated public interest and concern about how problematic CSR can be in terms of authorising corporate political meddling, and exceeding the proper purposes of companies.[29]

However, such commentary — which is typified by calls for companies to stick strictly to making money — has also generated more heat than light, especially about the strategies that might successfully curb corporate political meddling and stop CSR from becoming an ever more expansive justification for escalating involvement in politics.[30] One can only wish that curbing CSR — and supposedly returning business to a golden age when the business of business was simply business — was purely a matter of getting business leaders to learn their company law, read their Milton Friedman, and cease virtue signalling on company time.[31]

This book takes a more balanced approach to the subject. It begins by providing an alternative and nuanced account of the rationale for legitimate CSR activities, starting with an exploration of its origins and development. This reveals that there is merit in the 'business case' for CSR, with regards to effectively managing social risks to company interests.

In well-managed corporations, it can be reasonable and

realistic for company directors and managers to display social responsibility — as a matter of exercising good commercial judgement — towards the interests of a broader group of stakeholders, because such good practice occurs not at the expense of shareholder's interests but can protect and add to shareholder value.

However, the perspective employed here is still a critical one. In general — and beyond the 'culture war' analysis — CSR in Australia has been subjected to insufficient scrutiny. This is in part because in the debate inside business circles, discussion of the merits of CSR is usually confined to those who work in the 'industry' — either in the relevant company teams and divisions, or in the professional services and consulting sector. Hence the discussion generally tends to consist of companies being criticised for not doing enough CSR, while emphasising the supposed benefits of them doing more CSR by getting companies involved in social issues and political debates that have little, if any, connection to the genuine interests of shareholders.

Indicative of this — and of the activist mindset of many CSR professionals — is the 2018 Deloitte Global Human Capital Trends report. This survey of Australian business leaders, which was conducted by one of the leading business consultancies in the nation, found that only 23% said that "social responsibility is a top priority reflected in their corporate strategy." These results were not presented as raising questions about the priorities of a quarter of the corporate workforce, but rather as a "wake-up call" for Australian business that was "falling short when it comes to building a strategy to making a difference in society." [32]

An Institutional Response

This book draws attention to the issues that have been largely ignored. There has been relatively little consideration of the potential risks and negative brand and reputational consequences of escalating corporate involvement in CSR leading to companies ultimately becoming embroiled in politically-charged issues. The dangers of companies becoming inherently, inevitably, and inappropriately politicised are particularly relevant at a time when, as outlined here, moves to further 'mainstream' CSR at the heart of corporate governance gather momentum.

This even includes proposals to make CSR mandatory by changing company law, and have corporations participate in 'systemic' political change. This would revolutionise the role of companies, and give the CSR activists the license to play politics they seek.

This book therefore challenges the essential premise of the ideas being pushed by the CSR industry. In a free and democratic society, the notion that company names and good standing are enhanced by speaking out on questions unrelated to business interests and on which the community is divided is absurd. Pushing progressive causes that do not appeal to those with conservative views means that activities conceived of as socially responsible simply end up politicising company brands and reputations.

Public companies have special legal rights granted by the community. As a general principle, such companies should avoid abusing those privileges by getting involved in contentious social debates that will brand them as divisive political players. This is especially so at a time of growing polarisation in the community around cultural issues.

It is these aspects of CSR — the under-examined risk of politicisation associated with such activities for companies and the broader business community — that are focused on here.

The rhetoric emanating from the CSR industry about corporate involvement in political change should be a wake-up call for company boards, executives, and shareholders about where CSR is headed and the political risks this poses to the best interests of companies. However, business leaders and shareholders who might wish to challenge the well-established CSR doctrines and structures across business are not currently able to be guided and assisted by an alternative set of principles, practices, or frameworks to counter the 'industry' approach.

Simply complaining about the apparent takeover of companies by 'corporate lefties' achieves little, and does nothing substantive to prevent the CSR industry from playing fashionable cultural politics with shareholder's money. Hence to stop to the politicisation of Australian companies, this book proposes an appropriate institutional response. It suggests that the CSR activities of companies can be prevented from straying into political activism by introducing a new principle and new set of ground rules into the governance and management of Australian corporations — the Community Pluralism Principle. (See Chapter 4)

In essence, this principle would flag the need for companies to avoid the risk of politicisation by creating a new requirement for companies to respect the pluralism — the different views and values — of the community, which is impossible if they become 'political' in the name of CSR. It would require company directors and other decision-makers to limit CSR activities to ensure that involvement in social issues does not distract from company's core business mission and negatively affect its brand and reputation. Application of this principle would thereby hold business leaders accountable for preventing the politicisation of companies and stopping corporate virtue signalling from escalating into political meddling.

2

The Rise — and Rise — of CSR

Modern Attitudes to Corporations

The recent high-profile 'social responsibility' activities of Australian companies have created the misleading impression that CSR is a relatively new development. In reality, CSR has much longer history stretching back to at least the period after the World War II.

The rise of CSR — and its institutionalisation within business — is a product of intersecting international economic, social and cultural factors in contemporary society. In a more complex, more questioning, and more globalised world, factors such as the concentration of economic and political power and influence in large corporations, the greater emergence of counter-cultural attitudes towards established authority, and the growth of the international environmental movement, have all combined in

17

the marketplace of public opinion to shape how the community has expected modern corporations to be more accountable for their activities.

These developments have shaped the way modern societies have expected corporations to look beyond a narrow financial calculus and consider their business operations' environmental and social impacts upon society. This has included — as is implicit in the notion of a company's activities being subject to a social license — the expectation that corporations will operate transparently with regards to their conduct, such as by publicly reporting on their social impacts against environmental and other criteria.

International Developments: 1950s to 1980s

The greater community interest in the social role of companies has stemmed, in the first instance, from the powerful economic role corporations have played since 1945. The way the corporation emerged as the dominant form of private sector business organisation and vehicle for entrepreneurial activity in Western liberal-democratic capitalist societies invited and has led to greater scrutiny of corporate conduct. [33]

This scrutiny was motivated by the underlying social concern that the apparent political influence of economically-powerful corporations would be used to protect vested interests and subvert the public interest. The accompanying expectation that companies needed to be more open and transparent about taking responsibility and being accountable for the broader impacts of their activities was further heightened by cultural developments since the 1960s. Particularly, important was the growth of a strong and influential not-for-profit or non-government organisation (NGO) sector that has critiqued the performance of corporate entities actions and impacts across a range of environmental and social issues.[34]

In the United States, concerns about the social impact of large corporations wielding disproportionate economic and political influence began in the 1950s, and were intensified by the aggregation of corporate power through aggressive acquisitions and mergers from the early 1980s. The rise in the US (and elsewhere) of a corporate culture in which 'hostile takeover merchants' were often lionised as model capitalists led to concerns about the creation of market and shareholder value being prioritised over social considerations.[35]

Local factors have also played a role in European nations, such as the UK and France, where the privatisation of formerly state owned and operated utilities generated scepticism and additional scrutiny of the activities of corporations formerly in public ownership.[36]

Globalisation has also been a crucial factor in the rise of CSR, as the impact of multinational companies operating in developing nations led to criticism of corporate behaviour assessed against environmental, human rights, and labour standards criteria; and to the demand for greater corporate accountability to address corruption and exploitation.[37]

Green and Blue Collar Factors

The cultural expectation that companies should be held accountable for their social impact, and the belief that such scrutiny was warranted, has especially gained legitimacy through the flourishing of the international environmental movement over the last half-century.

Growing community concern about the depletion and the degradation of the earth's natural resources focused on the activities of the large corporations who were held chiefly responsible for 'exploiting' those resources for profit. The demand that company decision-makers take full account of environmental impacts was linked with an overall critique of corporate behaviour. This also betrayed a certain anti-capitalist mindset and aversion to the 'immorality' of the profit-motive, and was said to focus on the generation of profits in the short-term to satisfy the markets and shareholders, at the expense of long-term sustainability.[38]

This has led to the ubiquitous use of the term 'sustainable' in the CSR context to describe how companies seek to reduce environmental impacts and ensure their economic activities generate 'sustainable returns' over the long-term.

The priority given to sustainability has also been sharpened by global factors, such as the United Nation's focus on 'sustainable development' since the early 2000s, and by the emergence of several global indices (such as the Global Reporting Initiative (GRI) and the UN Global Compact[39]) that encourage companies to voluntary report on the environmental, social and economic impact of their activities against internationally recognised sustainability principles (the so-called 'triple bottom line').[40]

A substantial proportion of CSR activities therefore have a clear and proud 'green' hue as companies strive to prove their environmental credentials. In recent times, such activities have focused on the issue of 'climate change', as companies have sought to manage the 'carbon footprint' of their activities.[41]

However, as the debate about the social role of corporations developed in the United States in the 1960s and 1970s, environmental concerns were matched, if not exceeded, by concerns about the bread-and-butter economic impact of corporate activities.

These concerns arose in the context of the rise of corporate raiders and the social impact of hostile takeovers. The question that was posed by legislatures for directors of companies targeted for takeovers, was whether primacy should be given to shareholders' interests (and the economy-wide benefits), or whether bids should be assessed based on the impact of mass retrenchments and the closing or relocating of factories on small towns and local communities. This led to the legislating in the majority of US states of 'corporate constituency' statues. These statutes were designed to allow directors of targeted companies to reject hostile bids by considering not only the best, short-term interests of the shareholders, but also the long-term effect on the non-shareholder interest of employees, suppliers, and customers in the communities in which the corporation's facilities were located.[42]

These 'blue collar' kind of CSR initiatives — which actually allowed directors to take the other interests into account; but only to the extent of still acting in shareholder's best interests — had limited effect in reality. They have, however, taken on a new significance following the election of Republican President Donald Trump. Trump's campaign promise to revive manufacturing industry in America resonated with so-called white working class voters in economically-depressed states across the former manufacturing heartland of the mid-west of the United States.[43]

Explaining the Cultural Context

Critics who stick strictly to the culture war analysis of CSR — and who suggest that corporations have simply become another institution through which the left has marched — fail to appreciate the cultural context for explaining its rise.

Corporations cannot, do not — and should not — operate in a cultural vacuum. It is therefore reasonable to expect that a modern corporation's actions and behaviour will be influenced by the nature and character of the societies that house and produce them. This is illustrated by the way the range of 'counter-cultural' factors considered above has led to company's becoming more open and transparent about their economic, social, and environmental impacts.

It is also to be expected that organisations that trade on their reputations, such as public companies and other commercial enterprises, would strive to build trust by respecting and reflecting prevailing social and cultural values. These are commendable and socially-valuable cultural practices. They are consistent with conservative thinking about the role of culture. In properly self-regulating societies, individual and institutional actions and behaviour should be shaped in the public interest by established social norms and values.

One of the standard arguments for CSR is that customers and investors are making choices in an era when technology is providing an increasing amount of information about corporate responsibility. This includes a range of internationally-recognised corporate responsibility market indices that allow consumers to support products, brands, and companies that align with their values on a wide spectrum of issues, ranging from labour standards to the environment.[44]

As the federal government Corporations and Markets Advisory Committee's 2006 report on The Social Responsibility of Corporations realistically argued, balancing the economic role of companies with broader social considerations pertaining to other stakeholders is a legitimate subject of public interest. It is also ultimately a question that calls for the exercise of sound commercial judgement by company directors and senior managers responsible for corporate decision-making, given that:

> ... companies and those who govern their affairs do not operate in a values-free zone and their activities are and should be subject to evaluation and criticism. Within the marketplace of opinions, preferences and communication, the views and expectations of investors, employees, customers, local communities and other interest groups influence the way in which companies conduct their businesses and present themselves.[45]

The cultural explanation also points to the real — but underemphasised — problem that most critics have with CSR. This is that the expansive view of the socially and environmentally responsible business practices many companies take today reflects the left-wing progressive values that are culturally ascendant on subjects including 'diversity' and 'climate change'.

From this culture war perspective, the real 'problem' is that CSR is a symptom, or a product, of a culture that is dominated by left-of-centre perspectives in the culture-shaping institutions across the universities, arts, and media that play powerful roles in the production and transmission of social values. The character of CSR activities is also a symptom of other broader cultural currents: it reflects the fact that left-progressive activism and advocacy is more organised, better resourced, and purposeful —

it knows what it wants and how to get it including by shaping the CSR agendas of business — compared to conservative counterparts.

In Australia: 1990s to 2000s

The Australian business community was a relative late-comer to the issue of corporate social responsibility.

It was only in the 1990s that major local companies started to develop CSR policies. This was in part under the influence of globalisation and the impact of the 1980s reforms that opened the Australian economy to international business trends and practices including CSR. However, the emergence of CSR in Australia was also spurred by high-profile corporate collapses and scandals in the late 1980s, and then in the late 1990s and early 2000s.[46]

It is this confluence that has chiefly led to the perception among some advocates and commentators that most Australian CSR activities amounts, at best, to 'window dressing' designed to polish the tarnished image of corporate Australia.

Hence CSR proponents often characterise current CSR activities undertaken by Australian corporations as mere tick-box actions designed to burnish the reputation of company brands. The critics argue that tokenistic approaches to CSR can only be addressed by the 'mainstreaming' of corporate responsibility — by fully integrating social and environmental considerations into the normal internal business operations and the strategic and commercial decision-making processes and practices of corporations.[47]

The criticism is not without foundation; but nor has been the response by the business community to encourage a more meaningful approach to CSR, efforts which have been typified and led by the Australian Stock Exchange.

In August 2002, the ASX Corporate Governance Council was formed. The Council, chaired by ASX and made up of 21 business, investment and stakeholder groups, was tasked with formulating what would become the first edition of ASX's *The Principles of Good Corporate Governance and Best Practice*, which was released in March 2003. In 2006, ASX conducted a review, and following extensive public consultations, the revised second edition Corporate Governance Principles and Recommendations were released in August 2007. The third edition released in 2014 was completely re-written and re-ordered.

As the chair of the Council pointed out in his foreword to the second edition, "a decade ago, the term 'corporate governance' was barely heard... [but] today is a staple of the everyday business language and capital markets are better for it." The term corporate governance refers to the framework of rules and process that holds company directors and managers accountable to shareholders and the market. ASX's and corporate Australia's interest in the topic was a response to the corporate scandals of the late-1990s and early-2000s. The perceived need to develop a "practical guide for listed companies" represented an enlightened attempt at good self-regulation. It was designed to pre-empt heavy-handed government regulation by promoting "a high standard of corporate governance in Australia without the agency costs of 'black letter' law common in other markets."[48]

This motive was enhanced by the impact of the 2008 Global Financial Crisis. While Australian markets and financial institutions emerged relatively unscathed from the crisis in the US and Europe, the international trend towards new legislation regulating corporate behaviour heightened the incentive for Australian business to keep their governance houses in order.[49] This was reflected, in particular, by the attention paid to 'risk management' strategies, processes, and obligations in the 2014 version.[50]

A relatively new phenomenon in the corporate world, Risk Management, entails the development of internal processes and systems that identify, monitor, measure, manage, audit and report on company's exposure to financial risk that endanger the success of a business.

ASX's Governance Standards

The various versions of the ASX's best practice guidelines articulate many sound principles and practices to guide the behaviour of boards and executives, protect the rights and interests of shareholders, and promote accountable and transparent management of financial reporting, disclosure, and risk.

However, along with concentrating on the 'core business' elements of corporate governance, each iteration has not only included specific reference to CSR but has 'mainstreamed' corporate responsibility by presenting it as a core business feature of good corporate governance principles and practice.

This reflects the "evolving nature of the corporate governance debate".[51] The first edition had explicitly endorsed the standard rationale for CSR in terms of managing the "legal and other obligations to all legitimate stakeholders", and the "broader issue of enhancement of corporate reputation", while also endorsing the notion that CSR "can create value." [52]

The understanding of CSR as a genuine business proposition and part of the core business of good corporate governance — and as a responsibility of boards of directors — was fully endorsed in the revised second edition, which stated:

> To make ethical and responsible decisions, companies should not only comply with their legal obligations, but should also consider the reasonable expectations of their stakeholders including: shareholders, employees, customers, suppliers, creditors, consumers and the broader community in which they operate. It is a matter for the board to consider and assess

what is appropriate in each company's circumstances. It is important for companies to demonstrate their commitment to appropriate corporate practices and decision making.[53]

Tellingly, far greater emphasis was placed on social responsibility compared to the first edition, which was more focused on promoting ethical business behaviour by directors and executives.[54] This also encompassed promoting integration of CSR into core business and operational processes as a matter of recognising and managing risk.[55] Risk management not only included financial risks, but also non-financial risks relating to sustainability or social risks considered 'material' to the success of the business:

> Each company will need to determine the "material business risks" it faces. When establishing and implementing its approach to risk management a company should consider all material business risks. These risks may include but are not limited to: operational, environmental, sustainability, compliance, strategic, ethical conduct, reputation or brand, technological, product or service quality, human capital, financial reporting and market-related risks...When developing risk management policies the company should take into account its legal obligations. A company should also consider the reasonable expectations of its stakeholders.

Stakeholders can include: shareholders, employees, customers, suppliers, creditors, consumers and the broader community in which the company operates. Failure to consider the reasonable expectations of stakeholders can threaten a company's reputation and the success of its business operations. Effective risk management involves considering factors which bear upon the company's continued good standing with its stakeholders.[56]

Risk Management

Eric Mayne, the ASX Corporate Governance Council chair, has suggested corporate Australia largely supported the move to mainstream CSR. Mayne noted that while some submissions to the review process had raised objections to considering CSR in the context of risk management, the bulk of submissions were in favour:

> There is a clear message from submissions that concerns about [CSR] are a legitimate issue, and that they are not new. Companies should be encouraged to receive this message and it should be better reflected in the 'mainstream' of corporate governance activities, that is, through strengthened risk management processes and reporting.[57]

Consistent with a mainstreaming approach to CSR, the third

edition simplified the language but reiterated the 'material' or business case for CSR:

> A listed entity's reputation is one of its most valuable assets and, if damaged, can be one of the most difficult to restore. Investors and other stakeholders expect listed entities to act ethically and responsibly. Anything less is likely to destroy value over the longer term. Acting ethically and responsibly goes well beyond mere compliance with legal obligations and involves acting with honesty, integrity and in a manner that is consistent with the reasonable expectations of investors and the broader community. It includes being, and being seen to be, a "good corporate citizen"… Acting ethically and responsibly will enhance a listed entity's brand and reputation and assist in building long-term value for its investors.[58]

In addition, risk management and reporting for non-financial CSR risk was placed on a par with risk management and reporting of financial risk — in the wake of the GFC, no less — to address "the increasing attention being given by the investment community to environmental and social issues and the investment risks they raise." [59,60]

> A listed entity should disclose whether it has any material exposure to economic, environmental and social sustainability risks, and, if it does, how it manages or intends to manage those risks.[61]

According to the guidelines:

> How a listed entity conducts its business activities impacts directly on a range of stakeholders, including security holders, employees, customers, suppliers, creditors, consumers, governments and the local communities in which it operates. Whether it does so sustainably can impact in the longer term on society and the environment. Listed entities will be aware of the increasing calls globally for the business community to address matters of economic, environmental and social sustainability and the increasing demand from investors, especially institutional investors, for greater transparency on these matters so that they can properly assess investment risk.[62]

The third edition did not require companies to publish a sustainability report, and only mentioned that if such a report was published it could be cross referenced to meet the recommendation. This was in keeping with the 'guidelines' nature of ASX's 'corporate governance principles' which are non-binding on publicly-listed companies.

However, under ASX listings, companies are required to comply with a general governance disclosure requirement and include a statement in their annual reports declaring the extent to which they have followed the guidelines. This entails an 'if not, why not' approach, which requires that explanations be given for why specified guidelines have not been followed.[63]

Since 2014, companies must also lodge a detailed checklist ('Appendix 4G') of each recommendation and if not followed, an explanation of why not.[64] By applying a version of the tried and tested principle of 'what gets measured and reported, gets done', ASX has a created a mechanism — and a motive to take the line of least resistance and avoid the potential embarrassment of explaining why a company has done nothing to act socially responsibly — that encourages compliance and thereby shapes corporate governance, including deepening company's commitment to CSR. ('If not, why not' has also encouraged compliance by creating a mechanism for advocacy groups and activist shareholders to hold companies to account and exert pressure on boards and managers.[65])

In sum, the 'material business risk' approach recommended by ASX seeks to mainstream CSR into strategic decision-making and operational practices across all levels of company management — and not simply on the basis that well-managed companies should be responsive to relevant cultural and stakeholder considerations.

Nor does the recommended approach treat CSR as simply the transactional cost of acquiring a 'social licence' by factoring in the social and environmental impacts into corporate governance and management decisions. Rather than an 'add-on' — an incidental activity that could be characterised as either a cave-in to interest groups or as essentially philanthropic or promotional in nature — the business case for CSR insists these activities that consider the legitimate social and environmental interests of stakeholders are central to the overall business strategy and to the protection and creation of market and shareholder value.[66]

Merits of the 'Business Case'

The legislative and regulatory responses to corporate scandals have also played a role in encouraging companies to adopt CSR practices. These responses, both in Australia and internationally, have featured a raft of new accountabilities for company directors, which have principally involved compliance with new reporting, disclosure and auditing requirements. In general, the corporate governance culture that has developed is heavily focused on risk management and reduction.[67]

The 'business approach' to CSR applies — explicitly so in the ASX guidelines — what has become the accepted and well-established risk management practices the cornerstone of contemporary corporate governance across business.

At company board level, managing regulatory and financial risk and meeting the complex compliance obligations this entails, can create crowded agendas that detract from focusing on operational matters and new expansion and entrepreneurial opportunities. (Especially as company directors in Australia are subject to strict legal personal and sometimes criminal liabilities for corporate fault under various state and federal statutes.[68])

Focusing on CSR risk issues also looms as another distraction and displacement activity at both board and management level. Technical compliance requirements has "led to directors being swamped by hundreds of pages of board paper", and prevents time-poor boards from being able to focus on 'big picture' strategic and risk issues, including the proper management of the internal culture of companies.[69]

However, given the prevailing corporate culture, the business case for CSR transforms these social and environmental issues into another series of risks that call for the exercise of commercial judgement and foresight to effectively manage perceived non-financial risks to the company's commercial interests and the long-term success of the business.

This effectively elevates the importance of CSR based on the assumption that these activities do not merely boost corporate reputations in the community, but can also secure commercial advantages and add market value — such as by attracting customers, investors or employees, or by good environmental and social practice and self-regulation forestalling government intervention and potentially costly additional new regulation and compliance obligations.[70]

There is merit in the 'business case' for CSR: in well-managed corporations, it may be reasonable and realistic for company directors and managers to exercise good commercial judgement to effectively manage social risks to the company's interests in the best interests of shareholders.

Appropriate and Inappropriate Political Risks

It is therefore appropriate — as a practical matter of good management and under the heading of CSR — for companies to use foresight to address unsustainable environmental or other practices which, if unaddressed, may affect future shareholder value if such risks are not addressed. This might include continued participation in dying industries or exposure to future liabilities and damages.

This could also extend to activities that might address the externalities or future costs on society of a company's social impact, either through its use of resources or through the use of its products. This would be most appropriate in circumstances when the failure to address the companies' social impacts could foreseeably impact on shareholder's interests such as by impacting on brand or reputation, or by inviting government action that would negatively affect the company.

These kinds of reasonable and legitimate CSR activities conducted in the interests of shareholders may require companies to be involved in trying to influence political debates to encourage governments to implement, or not to implement, certain policies that are, or are not, in the best interest of the business.

However, CSR activities in Australia have courted controversy and criticism with respect to companies 'being political' over issues that appear to have little apparent connection to shareholder interests; notwithstanding the typical

CSR rhetoric and abstract appeal to earning a 'social license' by taking a stand on social issues important to stakeholders.

This was highlighted by corporate involvement in the marriage equality campaign. However, the issue now is that this example of corporate meddling in political debates may be just the tip of the politicisation of Australian companies, if the expanding 'industry' of CSR activists in Australian business achieve their objective and transform corporations into key participants in achieving 'systemic change' on contentious social issues.

3

The 'Industry' and the Subversion of Business

Professionalisation

The rising profile and acceptance of CSR as a legitimate part of corporate governance has been accompanied — and encouraged — by the emergence of CSR professionals within Australian business.

The professionalisation of CSR as a recognised field of business management is a result of the emphasis placed on mainstreaming and integrating social responsibility within normal strategic and commercial operations. It is also a natural product of corporate structures: when boards of directors and senior managers need assistance with new and emerging management challenges, it is standard practice to employ specialists as part of the corporate team to assume responsibility for those issues.

This has led to the deployment of considerable corporate resources to establish in-house CSR capabilities to manage the raft of new social responsibilities owed to stakeholders. This has been typified by the transformation and elevation within management structures of Human Resources departments — whose role and responsibility were formerly limited to employment practices — into 'People and Culture' divisions in charge of the formulation and implementation of corporate responsibility policies such as commitments to gender, sexual, and indigenous 'diversity'.

The professionalisation of CSR has also been marked, and encouraged, by the consultancy industry, particularly by the 'Big Four' professional services firms in Australia who are loud and proud about promoting their own CSR activities.[71]

Without necessarily challenging the integrity of those activities, the promotion of CSR by these firms could also be characterised as a 'loss leader', given that CSR has the potential to drive growth in new business such as external audits of corporate sustainability reports and on the consultant advice subsequently proffered to implement corporate structural and strategy changes recommended by the audit.

The contemporary corporate landscape is thus populated with internal and external actors with powerful and self-interested motives to promote and encourage the mainstreaming of CSR practices within companies.

The more CSR is treated as the core business of business, the more the allocation of larger amount of corporate resources can be justified — for such is the nature of the internal scramble over the allocation of scarce resources in bureaucratic organisations — to address these strategic and management issues; and the higher the status, authority and rewards in the corporate hierarchy can CSR professionals acquire.

An Insight into CSR

A clearer understanding of how CSR professionals advocate strongly for deeper corporate commitment and engagement with sustainability and social issues as part of 'core business' can be gained from the State of CSR in Australia report prepared by the Australian Centre for Corporate Social Responsibility (ACCSR).

Until it was (tellingly) absorbed by professional services giant Deloitte in November 2017, ACCSR was a consultancy specialising in CSR strategies. Its 2014 State of CSR report was based on a survey of almost 1000 respondents on the ACCSR mailing list. This was hardly a scientific survey. But the findings of the report — based on the self-selecting nature of the survey — illustrate the activist mindset of many of the CSR professionals that responded.

This mindset reflected the objectives and aspirations of

ACCSR itself, whose managing director argued in the forward to the report that the "professionalisation of CSR" is needed to extend beyond internal processes and operations because:

> It's not enough to do well at CSR any more. CSR leaders need to participate in systemic change, not just organisational change. Only in this way can we address deep-rooted social, economic and environmental problems to create lasting value for both organisations and their stakeholders.[72]

The notion that greater professionalisation should entail driving "meaningful change"[73] around social, environmental, and economic issues identifies the inherent — but under-examined — potential risks of corporate involvement in CSR.

Activist CSR professionals do not conceive of the professionalisation, integration and mainstreaming of CSR processes within business simply as means of ensuring companies effectively manage their social impact in the best interests of the business. Rather, the development of internal CSR capabilities and practices is conceived of as "the first steps of the journey" of enabling companies to participate in systemic change.[74]

This is to suggest that the business of business is to be actively involved in politics — an objective reflected in the (extraordinary) statement made by one survey respondent and prominently quoted by the ACCSR report:

For all the good work that's been done it still feels like we haven't made much difference. Minimal systemic change has occurred and the future under the current political climate seems very bleak.[75]

Other notable statements quoted included:

Sustainability made some real progress over the 2000-2012 period, but has travelled many steps backwards in Australia, very quickly. This is unsurprising; the electorate elected an anti-environmental government in Australia. Business [with few notable exceptions] has chosen to take advantage of this, and cut their effort, rather than taking the lead.

And:

Business is largely a laggard of regulation and has no incentive in Australia to promote sustainability values. Australia is dominated by a mentality of labour productivity and extracting value (from people and the natural environment).

And:

CSR in my area has stalled somewhat — is this due to economic or cultural or political factors — I don't know. There is no leadership on the issue — it's all about economics.

These quotes reveal a concerning outlook. It suggests that the ambition is that "buy-in" and "integration" of CSR into organisations will ultimately lead to contributing to systemic change, which will inevitably entail the politicisation of corporations. In the words of the report: "CSR will be strategic and action-oriented and make a real impact."[76]

Is the Business… Politics?

One international advocate has described this as the point at which companies seeking to promote collective action to address social concerns shift CSR "from being an object of civil activism to a key participant in civil society initiatives and processes."[77] Or as Deloitte Human Capital Leader, David Brown, put this in relation to the alleged wake-up call delivered to business about "their broader role in society" by the 2018 Deloitte Global Human Capital Trends report:

> The focus is now clearly on business' role in society as a driver of change. Just look at the role they played in the marriage equality debate in Australia late last year … Companies' reputation, relevance, and bottom-lines increasingly hinge on their ability to act as good citizens and influence pressing public issues.[78]

On this understanding of the ultimate 'focus', the business of business will not just be CSR. Under the envisaged escalation and transformation of CSR activities, the business of business will be politics.

Other aspects of the ACCRS report also reveal the other elements of the same outlook and ambitions. The survey found CSR professionals felt that while progress had been made, it had been slow, insufficient and focused internally. The suggested ways to hasten progress were to enhance engagement with stakeholders across multi-sectors, and improve reporting accountabilities beyond brand and reputation management.[79]

With respect to the latter, the report stated: "Respondents also hope that CSR will have more government support and that mainstreaming would be assisted by more mandatory CSR actions."[80] With respect to the former, the notion that respondents wanted CSR to entail "developing multi-stakeholder partnerships on issues of common interest" employs, inappropriately, the language and concepts of politics and coalition-building. This notion of stakeholder engagement goes beyond a process of establishing relationships to create internal awareness of the importance of CSR to the business.

The aims and objectives of CSR professional activists therefore indicates a process of internal subversion — diversion of companies from traditional business endeavours towards open political activism. Moreover, internal subversion and political activism begins with the support from respondents for government action to "increase mandatory requirements and create an enabling policy environment" for CSR strategy, reporting standards and more.[81]

Mandatory Social Responsibility

Within Australian corporations there is an influential and mobilised group of activist professionals — occupying strategic and important positions within the management structure — who are not only able to shape internal CSR practices, but also the official attitude companies take to external debates about corporate governance; both when engaging with government, and in business forums such as ASX and the AICD on these matters.

There is also an influential lobby of professional CSR activists in favour of mandatory government regulation of company CSR governance and management practices, whose potential influence includes shaping (or 'capturing) company's official attitudes towards and appetite for mandatory CSR.

The question of introducing mandatory CSR requirements — specific legal obligations for companies and legislative protections for stakeholder interests — into corporation law was considered extensively as part of the 2006 Corporations and Markets Advisory Committee report.[82]

This started with establishing the current state of the law, and initially by asking whether CSR — in terms of company directors and managers taking the interests of stakeholders into consideration — was legal. These legal questions pertaining to the primacy of shareholder interests have also been raised by

Corporate Virtue Signalling

critics of increased corporate involvement in social debates, such as Sydney's Catholic Archbishop, Anthony Fisher.

In a speech to the Sydney Catholic Business Network in April 2017, Fisher (a former commercial lawyer) asked whether the directors and managers of corporations were breaching their common law and statutory fiduciary duties — the "responsibility to shareholders to purse only the proper purposes of the company and to maximise profits within reason". Or were they abusing company's commercial powers and misusing company resources under the Corporations Act by becoming involved in social issues and political debates "on matters unrelated to the purposes of the business."

> In our polity, corporations enjoy various privileges such as legal personality and perpetuity, limitation of liability, corporate tax rates, protections of intellectual property and bankruptcy law et cetra, on the understanding that they will use those advantages for their well-understood commercial purposes, and not so as to become a Fifth Estate governing our democracy.[83]

Fisher's views are a powerful reminder of the principal purpose of companies — and a reminder that the primary duty under company law owed by directors and managers is, and should always be, protecting and adding value for shareholders. But is CSR legal or illegal?

Legal or not?

The Corporations and Markets Advisory Committee directly answered the question of whether CSR was legal under company law.

After reviewing the relevant provisions of the Corporations Act and the related common law cases and judicial interpretations, the Committee concluded that companies, with the respect to the duties of directors, "have considerable discretion concerning the interests they make take into account in corporate decision-making, provided their purpose is to act in the interests of the company as a whole, interpreted as the financial wellbeing of the shareholders as a general body."[84]

This is to say that, under the law, CSR was legal; consistent, at least, with a 'material business risk approach'. Under the standard 'principal-agent' model and analysis of the legal relationship between directors and shareholders, shareholders (the owners of the corporation) delegate the power to manage their equity interests in the company to the directors, who then delegate day-to-day decision making to senior managers under board supervision. However, the attendant duty of directors and managers to act in the interests of shareholders did not prohibit — and may require — "having regard to effects on other groups or social or environmental considerations that may bear on those ongoing interests."[85]

In practice, however, CSR may not always be in the interests of pursuing the proper commercial purposes of companies

This is significant when the commercial implications can be major. For example: with regards to financial institutions, fear of being 'named and shamed' by stakeholder and activists groups has resulted in the implementation of so-called ESG (Environmental, Social and Governance) 'responsible' investment and lending strategies.[86]

High-profile campaigns led by environmental organisations and the 'ethical' investment industry targeting financial institutions have led to all four major Australian banks (ANZ, NAB, Westpac and Commonwealth) committing to either cease or reduce lending to coal projects within Australia, ostensibly in the name of managing the long-term business risk of climate change abatement.[87]

Nevertheless, the courts have decided directors and managers are lawfully able to exercise a considerable discretion regarding CSR, and still lawfully fulfil their fiduciary duties. Legally, this is a practical question of commercial judgement — of making rational and reasonable decisions in good faith, and in the interests of, and benefit for, the company and the financial wellbeing of shareholders.

Under the law, the exercise of this discretion and use of company powers for a "proper purpose" might properly extend beyond short-term market considerations to the considerations of other interests relevant to long-term sustainability and commercial interest. This includes consideration of the interests of relevant stakeholders such as employees (in the interests of staff wellbeing and productivity), suppliers, and the broader impact of company policy on the community.[88]

Small Mercies

The significance of the findings of the Corporations and Markets Advisory Committee regarding the state of company law did not lie in ruling out any claim that CSR activities are inherently illegal and against director's duties and shareholder's interests. Its real, and more important, significance was that the Committee's report used the flexibility allowed by the current law to argue against the calls made for mandatory CSR provisions — for government regulation and legislation to explicitly clarify and define the extent to which directors may consider the interests of specific classes of stakeholders and the broader community.[89]

This aspect of the report reflected the terms of reference drawn up by the Howard Government, in response to self-evident 'industry' lobbying in favour of mandatory CSR (as part of the broader governance debate in the wake of corporate scandals). Hence the inquiry was commissioned to consider "the extent to which the duties of directors under the Corporations Act 2001 should include corporate social responsibilities or explicit obligations to take account of the interests of certain classes of stakeholders other than shareholders."[90]

This betrayed the influence and pressure of the activists

intent on mainstreaming and integrating mandatory CSR (and international developments such as the creation of ministries to promote CSR in the UK and France). The Committee was also asked to clarify not only "whether the current legal framework allows corporate decision makers to take appropriate account of the interests of persons other than shareholders". It was also required to examine if "there may be a positive role for Government to play in promoting socially responsible behaviour by companies" including "should the Corporations Act be revised to require directors to take into account the interests of specific classes of stakeholders or the broader community when making corporate decisions."[91]

The Howard government's attitude to these questions was confirmed by the government-controlled parallel inquiry by the Parliamentary Joint Committee on Corporations and Financial Services, whose June 2006 report, Corporate responsibility: managing risk and creating value, recommended against any changes to provisions concerning directors' duties.[92]

The Corporations and Markets Advisory Committee also recommended against any revision of directors duties in the Corporations Act — and herein lay the real significance of its report's clarification of the current law with regards CSR.

The Committee's finding that the "established formulation of directors' duties allows directors sufficient flexibility to take relevant interests and broader community considerations into account" clarified that CSR was legal, and government action to clarify and expand the law was therefore not needed. But more importantly, the aim and purpose of clarifying the law was to forestall the proposed changes to company law, which for the reasons the committee explained, would establish a much worse situation with respect to the potential nature and scope of CSR activities.[93]

The Committee warned that the general approaches suggested with regards to revising the Corporations Act and clarifying the social responsibilities of directors — by either elevating the interest of other groups on a par with shareholders, or by including an explicit statement of the other interests for directors to consider — would radically change company law and director duties.

This is because such changes would make it legal for directors to serve a wider range of stakeholder interests — whether defined or not — which would not be, as under current law, subordinate to promoting the interests of shareholders.

Allowing directors to refer to the competing or conflicting interests of stakeholders would, in effect, free them from — and render meaningless and unenforceable — their hitherto overarching fiduciary and legal duties to shareholders and creditors under criminal and civil law. It would leave directors with vague but a very wide and potentially unlimited discretion, which would leave them effectively unaccountable to shareholders for decision-making in relation to 'other interests' ... a law unto themselves "beyond the effective control of shareholders."[94]

What the Committee foreshadowed was not only a situation that, by making CSR mandatory, would revolutionise corporate governance for the worse. It also envisaged a situation that would make not only the current law, but also the 'business case' for CSR look like small mercies — tethered as it is under current law to the exercise of commercial judgement, an enlightened view of long-term company interest, and responsiveness to changing market and cultural expectation, but with primacy given to acting in the best interests of shareholders generally.[95]

Herein lies the strong case for resisting all efforts to make CSR mandatory — as recommended to the Committee by a number of submissions from environmental, ethical investment, and other stakeholder groups including ACCSR.[96] Any change to the law allowing directors to "give effect to non-shareholder interests for their own sake",[97] would amount to giving corporations what the CSR professional activists seek — a license to play politics and be a key participant in systemic change.

On the other hand, this also means that attempts to have CSR ruled illegal under the current company law could prove counter-productive — since if a legal challenge succeeded, this would inevitably fuel the campaign for mandatory CSR. This would occur at a time when the 'industry' push in this direction has already been renewed.

This has taken the form of calls for the Australian government to introduce a new legal framework to allow companies to strive for "equality and equity in business" and "create social, environmental, and economic benefit." This new corporate structure would take the form of giving companies the option of re-registering as 'benefit companies', requiring "company directors to pursue both profit-making and the public good, which considers all stakeholders in decision-making, not only those with financial interest in the company."[98]

No Political License

The latest attempt to make CSR mandatory should be resisted for the reasons set out by Corporations and Markets Advisory Committee with respect to the impact on directors' duties and accountabilities.

Moreover, mandatory CSR would inevitably allow and encourage the politicisations of corporations. Company directors and managers are not unelected politicians, let alone philosopher kings, possessing the requisite knowledge or wisdom to prioritise complex (and often directly opposed) competing interests and divine where the true public interest lies to solve social issues.

This is relevant to the ambitions and influence of the ethical or responsible investment industry. According to the CEO of trendsetting American investment firm, BlackRock:

Companies must ask themselves: What role do we

play in the community? How are we managing our impact on the environment? Are we working to create a diverse workforce? Are we adapting to technological change? Are we providing the retraining and opportunities that our employees and our business will need to adjust to an increasingly automated world? Are we using behavioral finance and other tools to prepare workers for retirement, so that they invest in a way that will help them achieve their goals?[99]

This is a very challenging definition of the 'social purpose' of companies. And beyond the question of whether companies have the means, let alone capacity, to 'make a difference' on such complex issues, it also begs the question regarding the role of business leaders. Surely it is difficult enough being responsible for the governance, management, and performance of large corporations, without also being expected to operate as an NGO-at-large responsible for curing assorted social problems.

On top of such practical matters, having to balance the competing interests of different groups in the community and find ways to reconcile those interests with the various compromises of those interests this will entail, is the job of politicians.

In his classic essay on the social responsibility of business, Milton Friedman went further when he described corporate 'agents' effectively making political decisions about the social role of companies outside of the rule of law as undemocratically usurping the functions and acting as "simultaneously legislator, executive and jurist." [100]

Or as a more blunt critic has put the same point about the usurpation of democracy differently: "Corporate social responsibility is no more and no less than an instrument used by non-corporates to gain leverage over corporations for political purposes."[101]

A more tempered version of this view was reflected in the Committee's wise advice that rather than politicise director's duties, it would often be a better approach to leave the resolution of conflicts between competing constituencies and protection of stakeholders interests — whether over social, environmental, or other issues pertaining to business practices — to parliament via "specific legislation directed to the problem area."[102]

4

Curbing Corporate Politicking

Implications for Boards and Senior Managers

Government action to regulate mandatory CSR requirements and practices should not be legislated because of the revolutionary and deleterious consequences for corporate governance. Nevertheless corporate decision-makers — along with the shareholders of public companies — need to be aware of how the ongoing professionalisation, mainstreaming and integrating of CSR into the corporate management threatens to politicise companies — without changes to the law.

Hence when exercising their managerial prerogatives and

commercial judgement concerning the CSR activities of companies, corporate decision-makers should be aware of three implications.

The first is that the foundational principles, logic, and practice of CSR — the notion that companies are part of society, and must therefore be responsive to social issues — encourage the escalation of CSR activities. Standard CSR practice invites lobby groups to engage with corporate entities to adopt and endorse their agendas, or risk the reputational consequences of a refusal by losing 'good standing' with stakeholders. CSR professionals see such engagement with stakeholders as their core role, and as integral to the process of mainstreaming and integration of CSR within operational and strategic management structures.

The second is that the notion that companies have a social responsibility to operate in the interests of a range of stakeholders can force companies to become publicly involved in social issues that appear to have only tenuous links to their business interests. CSR activities can hereby occur, and be justified beyond the obvious terms of any business case, in ways that inherently politicise companies' roles and brands by embroiling them in contentious political debates.

The third is that CSR therefore has promethean qualities that makes corporations susceptible to being drawn, perhaps unwittingly, into the 'culture war', and can lead, in practice, to corporate resources and influence being deployed in trying to achieve systemic change.

The standard CSR practice of engaging with external 'stakeholders' to discover the terms of their social licence makes companies particularly vulnerable to aping the 'progressive' political, social, and cultural agenda of activist organisations — in part due to fear of incurring reputational harm, via public shaming, if the activist's demands are not met. Such concerns have been heightened in recent times, when company brands are vulnerable to attack by activist driven social media[103] and shareholder activism campaigns around social and environmental issues such as divestment from fossil fuel industries.[104]

Given these new technology-enabled influences over corporate reputations and behaviour, it may be difficult for busines leaders to easily distinguish the difference between CSR activities that can be justified by a business case, and those that should rejected as inherently politicising. However, companies will find it more difficult to draw these distinctions and avoid politicisation unless the political risks associated with CSR are better understood and factored into corporate decision-making than currently appears to be the case.

Getting Out of the Bubble

With respect to identifying these political risks, business leaders will only perceive the dangers of CSR to company brands by getting out of their 'bubble'

When business leaders are encouraged by 'stakeholder groups' (invariably 'progressive' organisations and activists) and urged by their own CSR mangers to support a social issue — be it marriage equality, gender or sexual 'diversity', or climate change — they may feel they are simply acting in a socially responsible way.

But the reality is that companies are acting politically, [105] and are politicised, by taking sides on questions on which there is no community consensus. Business leaders may not realise this, and may think they are simply reflecting and responding to the position on these issues where society has already landed.

Such assumptions may also derive from — and reflect — the polarisation that is evident in many western countries (including Australia) between political, media, academic, and business 'elites' holding progressive views, and 'ordinary' citizens holding more conservative views, on issues ranging from religion and the family to immigration and climate.[106]

The evident community divide over social values suggests that business leaders would have to be politically tone-deaf not to realise that activities conceived of as socially responsible are inherently politicising of company brands and reputations; and that by embracing the values of some employees, customers, shareholders, and stakeholders they will be rejecting the different values and attitudes of other employees, customers, shareholders, and stakeholders.

Yet a key feature of the new social polarisation is that 'insider' elites — who work, live and socialise with other elites who think the same way — often don't appreciate that 'outsiders' think, speak, and act differently.[107] These divides are not just fostering social division and political polarisation; they are also undermining trust in political and other public institutions, such as universities, that are widely perceived to have embraced political correctness and virtue signalling over progressive social issues, at the expense of sticking to their core and traditional roles.[108]

Corporate leaders therefore need to be more aware of the political risks of CSR and the dangers of (heroically) assuming community consensus about the definition of socially responsible behaviour; especially at a time of significant political disruption and social fragmentation. This suggests that corporate decision-makers might be wise to discount the advice of CSR experts, and realise that in these politically uncertain times especially, CSR activities assume a new range of risks for companies that might find themselves at the centre of political storms.

The truth is that CSR incurs the risk, either wittingly or unwittingly, of involvement in contentious issues that can leave companies hostage to political fortune. These risks include the likely possibility that CSR will both foster internal political divisions and expose company brands and reputation to the external risk of politicisation; since not all employees, customers and shareholders — or stakeholders across the community — will agree about so-called responsible corporate behaviour regarding social issues in a free and pluralistic society.[109]

Keeping Companies Part of Civil Society

It is not always wrong for companies to assume a 'political' role in the context of the 'business case' for CSR, and in generally pursuing legitimate business interests. At times, it may be necessary for companies to try to influence political debates about contentious issues to pursue the best interests of the business.

However, when the link to shareholder's interests becomes faint, and the appeal to abstract notions of a 'social license' is used as justification for company actions designed to appeal to, or to appease, employees, customers, and other stakeholders, CSR activities become problematic in terms of companies 'being political', and results, in this sense, in companies becoming politicised.

A counter argument would be that companies becoming involved in political issues that are important to key internal stakeholders — such as employees and customers — may be in the interests of shareholders if the brand and reputational consequences help maintain or boost market share, or assist with staff recruitment and retention. The former may be true if, say, a company's market appeal is to a specific demographic. But that argument can hardly apply to the 'big corporates' —

such as banks, telcos, or airlines — that have mass markets and rely on broad consumer appeal.

Regardless of the generic CSR gloss that might be applied by insider CSR professionals to deny this, associating a company with a political position or world-view will inevitably repel dissenting employees, customers, shareholders and stakeholders from that brand. This outcome is hardly in the best interests of the company.

Some employees and consumers may want company brands to be aligned with their own values. It is a different question whether it is in the interests of company brands and reputation, let alone in shareholder's interests, to endorse and further encourage the hyper-politicisation of society, and support the values of some employees, customers, and stakeholders at the expense of the values of other employees, customers, and stakeholders. This is to say, that in relation to brand and reputation, as well as concerning market share and recruitment and retention, it is also in shareholder's interest to ensure companies remain pluralistic institutions; open to, and respecting of the rights and perspectives of, all groups.

The further, crucial, question is the appropriateness of customers, employees, and stakeholders demanding that shareholders' money be used to support their social and political views — and for company directors and senior managers to authorise the use of company resources for such purposes. This question should also be at the forefront of the minds of business leaders in response to the aims and objectives of the activist CSR professionals calling for companies to take on an overtly politicised role on 'pressing public issues' and 'participate in systemic change'.

Companies 'being political' by meddling in political issues for the sake of stakeholders' interests that are faintly, if at all, directly connected to shareholders' interests is the line that the CSR activities of Australian business should not cross.

Given that a legalistic approach to curbing CSR is fraught with danger, this issue should be addressed by company directors and senior managers through the existing channels of corporate governance. The potential escalation of CSR activities that threatens to lead to the politicisation of Australian companies should be addressed as part of good corporate governance as a matter of managing a genuine 'business risk'. A framework that could shape corporate governance, and guide and assist corporate decision-making in this direction, is outlined in the next section.

The Community Pluralism Principle

Corporate leaders who might wish to take a more sceptical and business-based approach to CSR will need to prevail in the inevitable internal management struggle over the CSR direction of the company. Unfortunately, corporate decision-making around CSR is not currently able to be guided by any alternative set of principles or policies, beyond reference perhaps to the 'business of business is business' mantra that is widely viewed as outdated.

Hard-headed corporate decision-makers who might wish to counter the well-established CSR management doctrines and structures that are now institutionalised across business, and combat both the activism and inertia of the CSR industry, are therefore at a disadvantage. This is due to the absence of anything resembling a counter-institutional framework to compare with ASX's pro-CSR governance principles, and help to shape and justify decisions taken to restrain and limit a company's CSR activities.

Ideally, this framework needs to be the kind of statement of directors and senior managers duties and accountabilities in relation to CSR that can shape and guide corporate governance and decision-making by being inserted at the relevant place into ASX's Corporate Governance Principles. It should also be the kind of statement that could be taken up by shareholders and shareholder organisations as a means of exerting greater authority over company directors and senior managers. If voted on at annual meetings and inserted into company constitutions, this would allow — a hitherto silent majority of — shareholders (who might wish to question what value is being generated by CSR divisions and activities) to tell directors and managers what the owners believe are the appropriate limits of CSR. It also needs to be the kind of statement to which companies, under the direction of their boards, might voluntarily subscribe to protect their brands.

A guiding statement of principle that could serve these purposes might be:

> It is important for modern corporations to consider their impact on all genuine stakeholders in the best interests of shareholders. It is also important that engagement on social issues cannot be perceived to distract from company's core business mission, duties, and accountabilities, nor negatively affect its brand and reputation in the market of opinion in a political sense. It is a matter for boards of directors and other corporate decision-makers to manage these risks by ensuring that companies respect and reflect the pluralism of Australian society and remain open to the views and values of all employees, customers, shareholders and stakeholders across the community.

The overarching purpose of articulating and disseminating such a principle would be to stem the politicisation of companies that might otherwise occur through the escalation of CSR activities. The principle therefore needs to overtly qualify and clarify existing CSR philosophies by flagging the need and importance for companies to avoid the attendant risks of politicisation. However, to be effective, the Community Pluralism Principle needs to take the balanced approach to CSR expressed in this statement.

Hence the principle, as drafted, reflects the essence of the current law that authorises CSR as a legal and legitimate area of discretionary management by boards and senior executives, when acting in good faith and in a reasonable manner for the benefit of the company. It also reflects the cultural reasons and realities why modern companies do — and should — consider the social impacts of their activities. It herein also embodies the business case for CSR as a matter of commercial judgement, and hence seeks to firmly link and limit CSR to considering stakeholder interests that are directly relevant to shareholders' interests.

However, it is thereby also expressly designed to rule out any question of CSR authorising participation in systemic change. In this vein, the principle is also crafted with the purpose of supporting and encouraging the view that decision-making around CSR should focus on managing the business risks of politicisation. The hope and expectation are, that by following the standard business language and practice of risk management, this may enhance the relevance and applicability of the principle to corporate decision-making, and thereby help facilitate its incorporation into corporate governance.

The 'Agency Problem'

The political risks entailed in professionalisation, mainstreaming and integration of CSR within Australian business are insufficiently flagged and discussed in the current debate and discussion about CSR. However, simply awakening corporate decision-makers to these risks is unlikely to be sufficient, of itself, to ensure the effective management of these risks and the curbing of CSR activities as judged appropriate.

A reason for this is that CSR activities can be subject to the 'principal-agent problem' that arises in public companies when directors and senior managers make decisions on the shareholders' behalf and allegedly in their best interests.

Given the intense and usually personal nature of much contemporary media scrutiny of corporate conduct, directors and senior managers — who are the 'public faces' of corporations — may have an incentive to use company resources to implement CSR initiatives that protect their individual reputations and improve their standing in the business and wider community by associating their personal corporate profile with 'worthy' social issues. In these circumstances, the agents who do not own the company impose all the costs of implementing self-interested CSR agendas on its owners: the shareholders.[110]

The 'agency problem' further helps explain the growth of CSR: directors and senior managers may be receptive to internal CSR agendas — and responsive to external stakeholder pressure — because they personally benefit, literally at shareholders' expense. Who actually benefits from CSR can be opaque due to lack of certainty and transparency as to the specific and overall financial benefits derived for the company that bears the administrative cost of CSR divisions, and the associated cost of CSR activities that supposedly protect the corporate reputation and standing of the company with stakeholders.

The principal-agent problem is one reason why external support and justification for sound, business-based corporate decision-making around CSR is needed to help business leaders and shareholders push back against the 'industry'.

Pushing Back

Another reason is the reality that in these polarised times, those who oppose 'progressive' CSR agendas risk professional repercussions and social 'death'.[111] This particularly applies within 'big corporates' in relation to attitudes to CSR, especially as People and Culture departments remain responsible for HR decisions related to hiring, firing and promotion. Subscribing to a set of social or political values should not be an employment prerequisite and represents a (normative if not legal) violation of the democratic rights and freedoms that all citizens should enjoy in Australia.

The criteria for employment and advancement should be what you can contribute to the mission of the company — not political criteria. Avoiding the politicisation of the workplace is a strong argument for curbing CSR. Yet the fact that quasi-political tests already play a role in employment practices —

in violation of the bedrock principles of a free society that respects the rights and freedoms of speech, thought, and conscience of all citizens — means that few in corporate Australia may be brave enough to openly challenge CSR orthodoxies.

A counter-institutional set of ground rules such as the Community Pluralism Principle would mean that directors, senior managers, and other members of corporate teams who want to limit the scope of CSR activities would not have to fight this battle based on the rights and wrongs of particular issues with all the risks this entails of being viewed as un-progressive. Instead, they would be able to refer to the need to ensure companies remain non-political as a general principle. They would not have to argue the case against a company taking a public position on the merits of an issue; they would only have to argue that the issue is political — with 'political' being a boo word — and therefore is a debate the company must keep out of to uphold its requirements under the Community Pluralism Principle.

Hence, it is unclear whether there is an appetite within the business community for curbing CSR, with one informed view being that most company directors and senior managers are generally either too timid or intimidated to speak up on this issue.[112] On the other hand, 53% of respondents to the Deloitte Global Human Capital Trends survey said social responsibility is not a focus for them.[113]

However, there has been some pushback by some corporate heavyweights against ASX's highly-politicising revised corporate governance guidelines. This indicates that business maybe slowly waking up to the danger posed by the abstract concept of a 'social licence' to the proper role and functions of companies.[114]

So perhaps — and notwithstanding the personal benefits that directors and managers can gain from implementing CSR — there is a silent majority in corporate Australia with a dissenting opinion, which is looking for something to say, and a way to say it, in order to push back against the CSR trend in business.

If there is an appetite for this, company directors and managers would benefit from being able to readily explain their decision by reference to an established, recognised, and counter-vailing rationale or principle; such as the Community Pluralism Principle.

5

Conclusion

Preventing Politicisation

Curbing CSR is not as simple as advising companies to 'stick to making money'. In a more complex world, and more complex business environment, considering the social impact of corporate actions is a legitimate part of the business of business. This is not only a legal and appropriate aspect of corporate governance; it is a matter of commercial judgement for company decision-makers to assess when the interests of wider groups of stakeholders need to be considered in the best interests of the business and shareholders.

However, the emergence of the CSR industry, and the mainstreaming and integration of CSR within corporate governance, poses genuine risks to companies and business in general. This includes not only the diversion of corporate resources into activities that, at best, can be considered marginal to the material interests of the business, and which can be justified only by applying the broadest definition of a CSR remit to protect the interests of stakeholders. The overarching risk is the diversion of companies from their core business mission into a political role, and the risks that politicisation and involvement in divisive social issues poses to company brands and reputations.

The risks associated with business being dragged into the culture wars are more acute at this time of apparent and growing community division over social values. The reputational risks of CSR also are that companies will risk being perceived as not only political players, but as agents of social and political division.

It might be, fairly, said that companies, being part of society, are simply reflecting the cultural polarisation that is occurring throughout society. However, public companies, given their special legal rights and privilege, should aspire to be pluralistic institutions that serve the whole community equally; which is impossible if companies acquire pejorative reputations for 'being political' by meddling in political issues for the sake of stakeholder's interests that are faintly, if at all, connected to shareholder's interests.

As the Hayne Royal Commission has reminded, the

greatest risk to corporate reputations, and the best way to protect those reputations, is to ensure that companies effectively and ethically fulfil their core business roles to benefit customers and shareholders. The Royal Commission has also illustrated the reputational damage that can be inflicted by engagement in social and political debates.

As this book was being finalised, the ASX announced that the proposal to introduce a 'social license to operate' into the new edition of the corporate governance guidelines had been abandoned. Instead the final version — reflecting the impact of the Hayne — has been updated to focus on corporate culture, and reminding companies of their duty to "instil and continually reinforce a culture across the organisation of acting lawfully, ethically and responsibly." Though the prescription that companies earn their social license by addressing issues such as tax minimisation have been dropped, elements of social engineering remain — particularly the new recommendation that companies have targets to address gender diversity.[115]

However, ASX Corporate Governance Council chair, Elizabeth Johnstone, denied having "run backwards" or "been afraid" to address the issue of social responsibility in the face of a backlash from business. According to Johnstone, despite support from "almost all investor interest groups, accounting bodies and standards setters," the Council had simply decided to substitute references to "reputation" and "standing in the community," which were "synonymous" with a social licence to operate.[116]

Johnstone's attitude suggests that critics of CSR should not take false comfort from developments that are anything but cause for complacency. The failure to resile from the social license concept, and the associated linguistic backtracking, bears all the hallmarks of a tactical withdrawal. It would be naïve to think the proponents of CSR will simply give up after encountering one setback.[117]

Averting Partisanship

This was confirmed in early March 2019, when union-backed industry superannuation funds — which control 36% of the nation's $2.7 trillion retirement savings pool — signalled their intention to purse an aggressive and activist CSR agenda. This strategy was announced by Greg Combet, the former head of the Australian Council of Trades Unions (ACTU) and Labor MP, who now chairs of Industry Super Australia and the industry fund-owned investment fund IFM Investors.

Drawing the wrong lesson from the findings of Hayne, Combet indicated that in order to rebuild trust in the wake of the Royal Commission, industry funds would use their power and voting rights as institutional investors to force public companies in the financial services, energy and other sectors of the economy to adopt an ESG approach to business and focus on environmental, social and governance issues, starting with climate change and "making a significant transition from old coal-fired power plants to renewable energy generation and distribution."[118]

This followed the decision by Glencore, Australia's largest coal mining company, to cap its coal production at current levels to abate carbon emissions, in response to pressure from investor activist group, Climate Change 100+, which includes the nation's largest industry fund, Australia Super.[119] It also followed the move by the ACTU and the Maritime Union of Australia to encourage 30 industry funds to use their leverage as shareholders to force BHP and Blue Scope Steel to guarantee the jobs of 80 seaman, and reverse the decision not to renew the contract of the last two Australian-crewed iron-ore carrying vessels.[120]

Concerned about the apparent distortion of the commercial decision-making process of industry super funds and of the companies targeted by CSR activism, the Treasurer Josh Freudenberg announced that he had written to the Australian Prudential Regulation Authority to urge it to consider whether it had sufficient powers to prevent union-appointed trustees with conflicts of interests from pursuing political objectives at the expense of their legal duties to protect members interests.[121] These are important questions; however, getting the regulators involved risks the counter-productive outcome canvassed above, by potentially opening up a debate about the need for government action to rejig corporate law and introduce mandatory CSR provisions.

These developments underline what has now clearly emerged as the genuine party-political nature of CSR — and hence the intensified risks for businesses concerned about politicising brands and reputations. The renewed push by the unions and their superannuation allies to use CSR principles to dictate how companies operate — to promote a political agenda — also shows that the (temporary) retreat on the language front by pro-CSR forces in business has not altered the fundamentals of the corporate landscape. The motives and methods of the burgeoning CSR industry that got us to the brink of ASX fully endorsing the social license concept remain unchanged — and, are arguably worse, given the way CSR principles are now being co-opted to advance a 'Labor' agenda, especially over industrial relations.[122]

The overtly partisan nature of the unions and industry-super funds CSR agenda underlines the importance of finding an effective way of ringfencing companies from politicisation in the name of CSR. This is also to emphasise that the distinctive characteristics of Australia's finance and investment sector — due to the union and Labor links of industry super funds — appears to make Australian companies more vulnerable to being led down the political path in pursuit of a 'social license'. Rather than be content with simply winning a short-term battle over ASX's governance guidelines — that will almost certainly have to be refought again in the future — those who genuinely wish to curb the role of CSR in Australian business need to focus on 'winning the war'. They should therefore fully support introducing into the language and practice of corporate governance an institutional framework and new set of ground rules — the Community Pluralism Principle — that embodies a sound and sensible approach to curbing CSR and promoting the proper role of companies.

Preserving True Diversity in a Free Society

Introducing the Community Pluralism Principle into corporate governance would not restore a golden age when business's business was business. Nor would it, of itself, guarantee that CSR activities are limited to legitimate business parameters, and do not extend into overt political channels — particularly when outcomes would continue to ultimately depend on the appetite among business leaders to challenge the thrust and momentum of the CSR industry (especially as the work of this industry may also add lustre to their personal corporate profiles at shareholder's expense).

However, at the very least, the rhetoric emanating from the industry about corporate involvement in political change — particularly in light of highly-political nature of the proposed ASX 'social license' guidelines — should be a wake-up call and generate questions at boardroom level about the willingness of CSR professionals to play politics with shareholder's money at the margins of what might be permissible under company law.

If the will exists to exercise some enlightened self-regulation — or that will is fostered by greater awareness of the business risks of politicisation — the ability to refer to the Community Pluralism Principle as an established part of good corporate governance might help curb CSR and prevent companies from inappropriately straying into politics; instead leaving the politics to politicians, parliaments, and the people.

This also indicates how corporate leaders could respond to institutional investors who seek to use companies to drive political agendas. The Community Pluralism Principle would provide both a shield and a sword to reject any use of CSR to force companies to undemocratically usurp the role of government in determining social and economic policy.

Moreover, if the Community Pluralism Principle was included in company constitutions at the initiative of a new kind of shareholder 'anti-activism' — by shareholders fed up with the diversion of company resources into political activism — it would send an even more powerful message about corporate political meddling. This would remind boards that shareholders — the true owners of the company — also hold diverse political views, and that some are sure to be unimpressed with company directors and senior managers using shareholders' money to play politics. By explicitly endorsing the Community Pluralism Principle, shareholders would make clear their opposition to corporate political meddling, in a way that would send an unequivocal signal that public companies should not cross the line between business and politics.

The overarching issue confronting business is the hyper-politicisation of society. This is the belief that everything is political — including the role of companies — and that all individuals and organisations need to take a stand. Business is caught in this vortex as CSR encourages companies to endorse 'progressive' causes, while alienating others who do not share those views. The choice for business is whether companies exacerbate hyper-politicisation by 'being political'; or whether they pursue the alternative path of choosing to remain part of civil society, which is where the Community Pluralism Principle leads.

Practising this principle would prevent the politicisation of companies by, ironically, allowing companies to practice the values of 'inclusiveness' that underpin many CSR initiatives that champion 'diversity' — but in new, important, and genuinely tolerant ways. By promoting respect for the perspectives of all members of the community, the Community Pluralism Principle would not only protect the fundamental rights and traditional freedoms of speech, conscience, thought, and association of all groups. It would also ensure that Australian corporations respect the only kind of diversity that ultimately matters in a liberal democracy: the diversity of political opinion that is the foundation of a free society.

Endnotes

1   Royal Commission into Misconduct in the Banking, Superannuation and Financial Services Industry, Final Report, February 2019.

2   'Banking royal commission: Hayne leaves out board accountability', Australian Financial Review, 4 February 2019.

3   Adam Creighton, 'Banking royal commission: Taxpayer and customer costs sure to rise from all this box-ticking', The Australian, 6 February 2019.

4   'Blueprint to strengthen banking, finance sectors', The Australian, 5 February 2019.

5   John Durie, 'Kenneth Hayne's structural shake-up falls short in the banking royal commission's final report', The Australian, 4 February 2019.

6   Jeremy Sammut, 'Business must keep firmly focused', The Australian, 2 January 2019.

7   For example, Tabcorp's annual Corporate Sustainability Review 2017 runs to 44 pages and cover 8 subjects from Economic Contributions to Environmental Data. Qantas's Annual Review 2017: Positioning For Sustainability And Growth runs to 33 pages and covers 11 major topics from Diversity and Inclusion to Climate Change and Environment.

8   'Qantas staff told to avoid 'gender inappropriate' terms like 'wife' and 'husband', News.com.au, March 4 2018.

9   'Qantas CEO Alan Joyce to campaign for Yes vote on same-sex marriage', ABC News Online, 21 August 2017.

10 'Same-sex marriage: Qantas commits', The Australian, 11 August 2017.

11 Alan Joyce, 'Why Australian companies and their CEOs should speak up on big issues', Business Insider, 22 March 2017.

12 The classic account of this view is Milton Friedman, The Social Responsibility of Business is to Increase its Profits, in Walther,Ch. Zimmerli, Klaus Richter, Markus Holzinger (Eds), Corporate Ethics and Corporate Governance, (Berlin Heidelberg: Springer-Verlag 2007), 173-178.

13 'Australian business leaders are pushing back against Peter Dutton's 'stick to your knitting' rebuke', Business Insider, 22 March 2017.

14 'Big business backs marriage equality campaign', Australian Financial Review, 22 March 2017.

15 "Stick to your knitting': Dutton tells CEO's to stay out of gay marriage', News. com.au., March 19 2017.

16 Or so is my impression gleaned from said members of the business community.

17 Judith Sloan, 'Royal Commission: Forget fuzzy feelings, give me boring bankers

any day', The Australian, April 24 2018; Joe Aston, 'Shared values: Only Black-rock's Pru Bennett understands NAB's Ken Henry', The Australian Financial Review, April 23 2018;

Aaron Patrick, 'Banking Royal Commission: The remarkable hypocrisy of AMP', The Australian Financial Review, April 20 2018.

18   AICD, '30 percent by 2018', 30 January 2019. http://aicd.companydirectors.com.au/advocacy/board-diversity/30-percent-by-2018

19   Judith Sloan, 'Rude light thrown on exclusive club of board directors', The Australian, May 5 2018; Janet Albrechtsen, 'Romantics and Utopians – A dream team to ignore', The Australian, May 9 2018.

20   This was dramatically highlighted when, in a bid to restore public trust and market confidence in the company brand, the board of AMP had to accept the resignation of its female Chair, who was widely perceived to be an 'affirmative action' hire, and who was replaced with one of the most experienced and respected male bankers in the country.

21   The Business Council of Australia had already led the way by supporting a 'voice to parliament'. BCA, 'Read Supporting Evidence': https://www.bca.com.au/evidence_indigenous

22   'BHP chief Andrew Mackenzie leads business backing for Indigenous voice to parliament', Australian Financial Review, 30 January 2019.

23   'Australian republic 'economically important' say business leaders', Australian Financial Review, 21 January 2019.

24   Review of the ASX Corporate Governance Council's Principles and Recommendations, Public Consultation 2 May 2018.

25   Janet Albrechtsen, Why corporate Australia should resist the Left's social engineers, The Australian July 25 2018.

26   "Stick to your knitting': Dutton tells CEO's to stay out of gay marriage', News.com.au., March 19 2017.

27   'Qantas staff told not to 'manterrupt' women', The Daily Telegraph, 5 March 2017.

28   Miranda Devine, 'Qantas language police on a power trip', The Daily Telegraph, March 6 2018.

29   Janet Albrechtsen, 'Why corporate Australia should resist the Left's social engineers', The Australian, July 25 2018.

30   Janet Albrechtsen, 'Romantics and Utopians – A dream team to ignore', The Australian, May 9 2018; Judith Sloan, 'Rude light thrown on exclusive club of board directors', The Australian, May 5 2018.

31   Janet Albrechtsen, 'Social activists have left a trojan horse at the ASX gate', The Australian, 29 August 2018.

32   'Australian companies are still slow to embrace social responsibility', Business Insider, 19 April 2018.

33   Corporations and Markets Advisory Committee, The Social Responsibility of Corporations, Report December 2006, 1, 16.

34   As above.

35   As above, 15-30.

36 As above, 15-30.
37 As above, 15-30.
38 As above, 20-1.
39 https://www.globalreporting.org/pages/default.aspx; https://www.unglobalcom-pact.org/_
40 The Social Responsibility of Corporations, 66-69.
41 For example, see Commonwealth Banks Corporate Responsibility 2017 report which includes "Our first Climate Policy Position Statement [which] outlines how we intend to support opportunities associated with responding to climate change."
42 The Social Responsibility of Corporations, 21-22.
43 As above, 100-102.
44 AICD, 'Responsible investing lifts governance expectations', https://aicd.com-panydirectors.com.au/advocacy/governance-leadership-centre/practice-of-gover-nance/responsible-investing-lifts-governance-expectations
45 The Social Responsibility of Corporations, iv.
46 As above, 32-33.
47 Stephanie Schleimer, John Rice, 'Australian corporate social responsibility re-ports are little better than window dressing.' The Conversation, October 4 2016.
48 ASX Corporate Governance Council, Corporate Governance Principles and Recommendations with 2010 Amendments, 2nd Edition (2007), 2.
49 ASX Corporate Governance Council, Review of the Corporate Governance Principles and Recommendations Public Consultations, 16 August 2013, 1-2.
50 'First anniversary of revised ASX Corporate Governance Principles and Recom-mendations', https://www.complispace.com.au/blog/financial-services-updates/first-anniversary-revised-asx-corporate-governance-principles-recommenda-tions/
51 Eric Mayne, 'Revised ASX Corporate Governance Principles & Recommen-dations', http://www.tved.net.au/index.cfm?SimpleDisplay=PaperDisplay.cfm&PaperDisplay=http://www.tved.net.au/PublicPapers/February_2008,_Law-yers_Education_Channel,_Revised_ASX_Corporate_Governance_Princi-ples___Recommendations.html
52 ASX Corporate Governance Council, The Principles of Good Corporate Gov-ernance and Best Practice, March 2003, 59.
53 Corporate Governance Principles and Recommendations with 2010 Amend-ments, 22.
54 See ASX Corporate Governance Council, The Principles of Good Corporate Governance and Best Practice, March 2003, 25
55 Mayne, as above.
56 Corporate Governance Principles and Recommendations with 2010 Amend-ments, 33-4.
57 Mayne, as above.
58 ASX Corporate Governance Council Corporate Governance Principles and Recommendations, 3rd Edition, 2014, 19.
59 ASX Corporate Governance Council, Review of the Corporate Governance

Principles and Recommendations Public Consultations, 16 August 2013, 2.

60 The disproportionate emphasis placed on social responsibility in corporate governance has also been a feature of critical commentary in relation to the Australian Institute of Company Director's Company Directors Course ⊠ which is the standard industry qualification for board membership. See Miranda Devine, 'Beware the Perils of Corporate Wokeness, The Daily Telegraph, 15 May 2018.

61 Corporate Governance Principles and Recommendations, 30

62 As above.

63 Corporate Governance Principles and Recommendations with 2010 Amendments, 2007, 5.

64 Corporate Governance Principles and Recommendations, 5.

65 'Is David Murray or David Gonski right on governance?', Australian Financial Review, 2 August 2018.

66 The Social Responsibility of Corporations, iii-iv, 40, 56-63, 78.

67 As above, 15.

68 AICD, Directors' liability for company actions: Duties of directors, https://aicd.companydirectors.com.au/~/media/cd2/resources/director-resources/director-tools/pdf/05446-6-11-liability-company-actions_a4-web.ashx

69 'David Murray's defiant plan for AMP', Australian Financial Review, 1 August 2018.

70 The Social Responsibility of Corporations, 41-47

71 'Corporate responsibility: It's time to accelerate the pace of change', https://www.pwc.com/gx/en/about/corporate-responsibility.html

72 Australian Centre for Corporate Social Responsibility, The State of CSR In Australia and New Zealand, Annual Review 2014, 3.

73 As above, 4.

74 As above, 5.

75 As above, 5.

76 As above, 7.

77 Simon Zadek, The Path to Corporate Responsibility, in Walther Ch. Zimmerli·KlausRichter Markus Holzinger (Eds) Corporate Ethics and Corporate Governance, (Berlin Heidelberg: Springer-Verlag 2007), 161-172, 168.

78 'Australian companies are still slow to embrace social responsibility', as above.

79 The State of CSR In Australia and New Zealand, 5-6

80 As above, 7.

81 As above, 9.

82 Wayne Gumley, and Helen Anderson,Corporate social responsibility: legislative options for protecting employees and the environment. [online]. The Adelaide Law Review, Vol. 29, No. 1, 2008: 29-77

83 'Catholic archbishop Fisher to CEOs: butt out of same-sex debate', The Australian, 1 April 2017.

84 The Social Responsibility of Corporations, 96.

85 As above, 81.

86 'Analysis: Is ESG a scam?', Funds Selector Asia, https://fundselectorasia.com/analysis-esg-scam/

87 'Big four banks slash lending to coal miners', Sydney Morning Herald, 24 July 2017.
88 The Social Responsibility of Corporations, 84-93.
89 As above, 81, 96.
90 As above, 3-4.
91 As above, 3-4.
92 Parliamentary Joint Committee on Corporations and Financial Services, Corporate responsibility: managing risk and creating value
93 The Social Responsibility of Corporations, 7.
94 As above, 97-98, 106.
95 As above, 111-113.
96 Corporations and Markets Advisory Committee, The Social Responsibility of Corporations: Summary of Submissions, December 2006.
97 The Social Responsibility of Corporations, 109.
98 http://bcorporation.com.au/blog/why-we-need-benefit-companies_
99 https://www.blackrock.com/corporate/investor-relations/larry-fink-ceo-letter)
100 Milton Friedman, The Social Responsibility of Business is to Increase its Profits, 175.
101 Gary Johns, Corporate Social Responsibility or Civil Society Regulation? The Hal Clough Lecture for 2002, Institute of Public Affairs.
102 The Social Responsibility of Corporations, 8, 97, 99.
103 'Coopers accused of homophobia after teaming up with Bible Society', Daily Telegraph, 15 March 2017.
104 'Commonwealth Bank says its lending for coal will continue to decline', The Guardian Australia, 16 November 2017.
105 It is also important to point out, in the Australian context especially, the genuine party-political nature of some CSR initiatives. For example, union movement and Labor Party-aligned 'industry' superannuation funds ☒ led by the peak industry body the Australian Council of Super Investors ☒ have been accused of bullying and abusing their power as powerful and influential institutional investors to force companies to comply with board gender quotas strategies. 'Chris Corrigan attacks business gender targets', The Australian, May 19 2018.
106 For the best account of these divisions, see David Goodheart, The Road to Somewhere: The New Tribes Shaping British Politics, London: Penguin Book, 2017.
107 Louise Clegg, 'It's not all about money: values expose broken political system', The Weekend Australian, 4 February 2017.
108 For an analysis of one aspect of these problems in the universities, see Bella d'Abera, The Rise of Identity Politics in History, Institute of Public Affairs, October 2017.
109 Jeremy Sammut, 'Public companies are already demonstrably diverse, why sign up to extra pledges?', Australian Financial Review, April 3 2017.
110 Nicolai J. Foss & Peter G. Klein, Stakeholders and Corporate Social Responsibility: an Ownership Perspective, Research Working Paper 2018-02, John F. Baugh Center for Entrepreneurship and Free Enterprise February 2018

111 Jeremy Sammut, Countering the counter-culture II: When ideology trumps reality, Policy, Winter 2016.

112 'Chris Corrigan issues a defence of capitalism during brief return', The Australian, 19 May 2018.

113 'Australian companies are still slow to embrace social responsibility', as above.

114 Janet Albrechtsen, There's a corporate rebellion brewing over fanatical social justice movements, Weekend Australian, 4 August, 2018.

115 ASX Corporate Governance Council, Corporate Governance Principles and Recommendations (the Fourth Edition), February 2019.

116 "Social licence' principle dumped', The Australian, 28 February 2019.

117 'Governance Council retreats on industry super's 'social licence' push', Australian Financial Review, 7 August 2018.

118 "Not activism': Industry super's plan to 'reshape' business for the long term', Australian Financial Review, 4 March 2019.

119 'Glencore moves to cap global coal output after investor pressure on climate change', ABC News Online, 21 February 2019.

120 'ACTU demands industry funds act against BHP', Australian Financial Review, 22 February 2019.

121 'Treasurer's super war on activists', The Australian, 4 March 2019.

122 'Unionist vows no retreat on IR super activism', The Australian, 5 March 2019.

Lightning Source UK Ltd.
Milton Keynes UK
UKHW021333160919
349872UK00015B/3672/P

9 781925 826432